Grant Wood

The Artist in the Hayloft

Prestel

Let's visit Grant Wood!

There he is standing by his paintings.

Hey, Grant. What town is that?

Who's riding the horse?

What's happening there?

What's with the funny hat?

We chatter.

Grant smiles and says...

2

...does it really matter?

Every small town is somebody's universe.

Grant Wood was a famous American artist. He was born on a farm near Anamosa, Iowa, and spent his first ten years growing up there. As a child, he taught himself how to draw. As an adult, he painted the things he knew and liked from his childhood—backyards and barnyards, houses and sheds, chickens, trees, and flowers. And windmills—he really liked windmills! How many of them can you find in the painting?

Even though Grant studied art in the big cities of Minneapolis, Chicago, and Paris, he always came back to his rural roots. In Stone City where he taught budding artists in the summer, Grant encouraged them to paint the people, places, and things of their own universe.

Every house is somebody's home.

Grant Wood was not the only famous person from Iowa. America's thirty-first President, Herbert Hoover, was born in a small cottage in the town of West Branch, not far from the Wood family farm. Both men grew up in families of Quaker faith, both were poor, and both became famous during the Great Depression. When he was ten, Grant's father died and his mother moved his family to Cedar Rapids. When Grant's mother could no longer afford to own her house, he built her a cottage, similar to the one seen here in Grant's preliminary drawing for his painting. Can you spot the differences between the drawing and the painting?

Somebody's junk is another's bouquet.

Grant Wood had many friends. They helped him by buying his art. One friend gave him a place to make his art—a hayloft above a garage. Another friend asked him to make a portrait of his house to hang over the fireplace. Grant thanked his friends by giving them a sculpture made to look like a bouquet of flowers. With a few scrap bits of metal and some household objects, he could make art out of things that would make you say

ouch!

Give him a pencil or paintbrush and he could make flowers that looked real to the touch.

8

Somebody's hat can do all the talking.

You can look at a painting by Grant Wood and say, "that's a farm," or, "a farmer," or "a chicken." You can look again and ask, "What was the artist trying to say?" By the way he dressed his characters—a farm woman, a city woman, an awkward adolescent fowl with two hens at his side—you can guess who is who in the story and what they might be thinking.

Grant let the speckled Plymouth Rock hen roost in his studio overnight so she could pose for him during the day.

ADOLESCENCE

Seems like they don't have much to say.

Grant saw the pointed window of a small house in the country and imagined a stern-looking couple with a pitchfork in front of it. The picture he went on to paint immediately made him famous.

Would you have guessed that it is a picture of Grant's sister and his dentist? Their pose, their clothes, and the pitchfork became symbols of simple rural life. They appear everywhere—in art, in advertising, in television, and the movies.

Somebody's in an awful hurry.

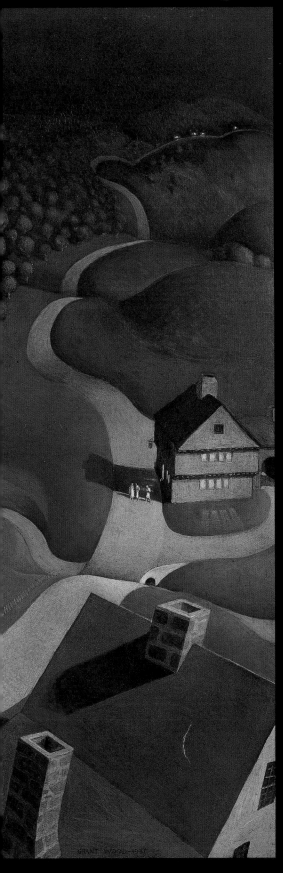

Grant was inspired by stories from history. He liked the one about the American revolutionary war hero, Paul Revere, who rode through the night warning his friends and neighbors, "the British are coming!" Grant composed this birdseye-view scene of the ride set in an imaginary small town.

If he needed a prop that was too big for his studio, he would use a toy version instead. Painting the galloping steed in the picture as a rocking horse was his own little joke.

Somebody's got some explaining to do.

Another story, told by a man named Parson Weems, was about America's first president George Washington as a boy. Grant placed the dollar bill face of the mature president on the body of the young truth teller as a funny way to say that even when he was young the future president was already great.

Notice what Grant used for trim on the edge of the curtain. What do you think is happening in the background of the painting?

Grant's humor also comes out in the inscription, "The Way of the Transgressor is Hard," on the wooden bench he made for his students—perhaps for those who could not tell the truth!

PARSON WEEMS' FABLE

This could be anybody's mother, sister…

His mother and sister always encouraged Grant's interest in art. When he was a boy his mother gave him sticks of charred wood from the stove to use like charcoal to draw with. His sister Nan, also an artist, helped him find props. Grant used color to create light and shadow in his realistic portraits and landscapes. He used half a potato dipped in black to stamp out the dark, circle shapes on his sister's blouse.

...friend,

aunt...

Grant made use of many kinds of shapes and lines in his art. He liked the designs made by the zigzig of rick rack, the squares in a checked pattern, or the diamonds in a plaid knit.

He was inspired by the personality expressed in clothes as much as that of a person's pose.

He used family photos, like this one of his aunt Tillie, to paint this Victorian woman. The shape of the telephone mimics her long neck.

ARBOR DAY

GRANT WOOD 1932

...You

Me...

Grant depicted his memory of a family meal at harvest time. It is set as if on a theatre stage and was so detailed that if larger it could easily fill a wall, like a mural. Even the shadows under the chickens were measured true to life. Any one of the boys or men could be the artist himself—wearing his favorite bibbed overalls, working hard, comfortable, and proud of his work and his universe.

The Life of Grant Wood

Grant Wood was born February 13, 1891, on a farm in the Midwestern state of Iowa. He spent the first ten years of his life in the company of his two brothers, a baby sister, his parents, his aunts, and a hired hand. He helped with chores, walked to school, and rode on horseback to the nearby town. He liked to draw and made art with objects that he found, like charcoal sticks from the kitchen stove. He closely observed everything around him—things from nature, buildings, his family. At age ten he made a list of 55 birds that he submitted to the local newspaper. At age 14 he submitted a lifelike drawing of oak leaves to a national contest and won third prize. In 1901, Grant's father died and the family moved from the farm to the nearby town of Cedar Rapids. Wood traveled the world but always remembered his rural roots.

Grant Wood, 1920s

Grant Wood at age 19

Grant Wood with McKinley Junior High School art students

Wood taught himself to draw. In high school he excelled in art classes and read magazines that taught him to draw and to make crafts. After high school, he studied metal crafting and picture composition at a school in Minneapolis, life drawing at the local university and a museum in Chicago and, later, painting in Paris. Besides drawings, his early works were jewelry, wrought iron hardware and copper wear, wooden furniture, and impressionist paintings— landscapes of Iowa, street scenes of Paris, and still lifes of flowers brought to the mortuary next door. He also made portraits. In 1930, Grant Wood won a prize for his most famous painting, *American Gothic*. Throughout his forties, he was known for promoting a realistic style of painting and regionalist (in his case rural Midwestern) subject matter. He was also known for his humorous take on American fables, traditions, culture, and society.

Wood was always close to his family. His father was strong and quiet and his mother loving. His sister Nan adored him. When times were tough, the artist always made room for his mother and sister in his home. He built two houses for them and himself and eventually they lived with him in his converted hayloft studio where he made his most famous paintings. Grant married late, after he became famous. His mother died shortly after that. Grant divorced his wife after only two years and, a little later, died from cancer in 1942, the night before his 51st birthday.

Grant Wood, c.1926

Wood was an artist, but he was also a teacher and lecturer and, during World War I, a soldier. He is famous for his paintings and for being a strong supporter of an artistic style. He is also known as a man who was gentle, funny, and kind.

The Studio

For ten years (1924–34) Grant Wood lived in a converted hayloft, above a garage, in his hometown of Cedar Rapids, Iowa. It was just before and during the Depression; his mother Hattie and sister Nan sometimes lived with him. Located in an alley off a main street, the loft comprised a kitchen, a bathroom, a bedroom, and a great room with skylight that took up most of the second-floor space. The first floor was a place for horses and hearses used by the artist's patron, a mortician. Wood gave his hayloft-turned artist's studio the fictional address, 5 Turner Alley. Here he painted his most famous paintings, including *American Gothic*.

Grant used his craftsmanship to make his loft into a workday space and a hideaway home. He built clever cubbies and niches to hold plants and collectibles, under-counter coves to hide rollaway beds, built-in drawers to put away clothes. He covered cupboard doors with old denim overalls to store his mother's fancy dishes and supplies. He constructed a pass-through from the kitchen to the dining nook, and a drop-down wall for privacy to the one bedroom. In this way and at different times, Grant used the loft to eat, and then to sleep, to do house work, and then to do artwork. He could bring out his supplies and work by the window's light by day, hide it all away, draw back the "stage curtain," and welcome as many as 50 friends at night to watch a play.

5 Turner Alley, north view

Interior view of 5 Turner Alley

"Mother's Hot Dog Stand" at 5 Turner Alley

The Pictures in this Book

All artworks are by Grant Wood unless otherwise noted.

Front Cover:
Young Corn (detail), 1931. Oil on Masonite panel, 24 x 29⅞ in. Cedar Rapids Museum of Art, Community School District Collection. 1930.35

Back Cover:
Study for *Self Portrait*, 1932. Charcoal and pastel on paper, 14½ x 12 in. Cedar Rapids Museum of Art, Museum purchase. 93.11

Title pages:
5 Turner Alley Christmas Card (detail), 1927. Relief print with hand coloring, pen and ink, 10 x 7¼ in. Cedar Rapids Museum of Art, Gift of John B. Turner II. 81.17.4

Page 2:
Door to 5 Turner Alley, 1924. Painted wood, fabric, glass, and wrought iron, 78 x 29⅞ x 1¼ in. Cedar Rapids Museum of Art, Gift of Harriet Y. and John B. Turner II. 72.12.15

Page 3:
Grand Wood with *Daughters of Revolution* at 5 Turner Alley, 1932. Cedar Rapids Museum of Art Archives.

Page 4:
Stone City, Iowa, 1930. Oil on wood panel, 30¼ x 40 in. Joslyn Art Museum, Art Institute of Omaha Collection. 1930.35

Page 5:
Grant Wood as a young artist, 1910. Cedar Rapids Museum of Art Archives.

Page 6:
Study for *The Birthplace of Herbert Hoover*, 1931. Charcoal, chalk, and graphite on tan paper, 29⅜ x 39⅜ in. The University of Iowa Museum of Art, Gift of Edwin B. Green. 1985.92

Page 7:
The Birthplace of Herbert Hoover, 1931. Oil on Masonite, 29⅝ x 39¾ in. Des Moines Art Center Permanent Collections; Purchased jointly by the Des Moines Art Center and The Minneapolis Institute of Arts, with funds from the Edmundson Art Fund, Inc., Mrs. Howard H. Frank, and the John R. Van Derlip Fund. 1982.2

Page 8:
Overmantel Decoration, 1930. Oil on upsom board, 41 x 63½ in. Cedar Rapids Museum of Art, Gift of Isabel R. Stamats in memory of Herbert S. Stamats. 73.3

Page 9:
Lilies of the Alley, 1925. Ceramic, paint, wire and found objects, 12 x 12 x 6½ in. Cedar Rapids Museum of Art, Gift of Harriet Y. and John B. Turner II. 72.12.38

Page 10:
Appraisal, 1931. Oil on composition board, 29½ x 35¼ in. Dubuque Museum of Art, Courtesy of the Carnegie-Stout Public Library, acquired through the Lull Art Fund. LTL.99.08

Page 11:
Adolescence, 1940. Oil on Masonite panel, 20⅜ x 11¾ in. Abbott Laboratories.

Page 12:
American Gothic, 1930. Oil on beaverboard, 29¼ x 24⅝ in. Friends of American Art Collection, all rights reserved by the Art Institute of Chicago and VAGA, New York, NY.

Page 13:
American Gothic House in Eldon, Iowa. State Historical Society of Iowa, Iowa City. Photo: Jan Nash.

Page 14:
Midnight Ride of Paul Revere, 1931. Oil on composition board, 30 x 40 in. The Metropolitan Museum of Art, Arthur Hoppock Hearn Fund, 1950. (50.117). Photograph © 1988 The Metropolitan Museum of Art.

Page 15:
Grant Wood with his unfinished painting, *Midnight Ride of Paul Revere*, at 5 Turner Alley, 1931. Courtesy of Figge Art Museum, Grant Wood Archives. Photo: John W. Barry.

Page 16:
Mourner's Bench, 1921–22. Oak, 37 x 49 x 16 in. Cedar Rapids Museum of Art, Cedar Rapids School District Collection.

Page 17:
Parson Weems' Fable, 1939. Oil on canvas, 38⅜ x 50⅛ in. Amon Carter Museum, Fort Worth, Texas. 1970.43

Page 18:
Woman With Plants, 1929. Oil on upsom board, 20½ x 17⅞ in. Cedar Rapids Museum of Art, Museum purchase. 31.1

Page 19:
Portrait of Nan, 1933. Oil on Masonite, 34½ x 28½ in. Chazen Museum of Art, University of Wisconsin-Madison, Collection of William Benton. 1.1981

Page 20:
Victorian Survival, 1931. Oil on composition board, 32½ x 26¼ in. Dubuque Museum of Art, Courtesy of the Carnegie-Stout Public Library, acquired through the Lull Art Fund. LTL.99.09

Matilda Peet, tintype, 3½ x 2⅛ in. Courtesy of Figge Art Museum, Grant Wood Archives.

Page 21:
Plaid Sweater, 1931. Oil on Masonite, 29½ x 24⅛ in. The University of Iowa Museum of Art, Gift of Melvin and Carole Blumberg and Edwin B. Green through the University of Iowa Foundation. 1984.56

Page 22:
Arbor Day, 1932. Oil on Masonite panel, 24 x 30 in. William I. Koch Foundation.

Page 23:
Boy Milking Cow, Fruits of Iowa mural for Hotel Montrose, 1932. Oil on canvas, 71¼ x 63¼ in. Collection of Coe College, Cedar Rapids, Iowa, Gift from the Eugene C. Eppley Foundation.

Farmer's Wife With Chickens, Fruits of Iowa mural for Hotel Montrose, 1932. Oil on canvas, 71¼ x 49 in. Collection of Coe College, Cedar Rapids, Iowa, Gift from the Eugene C. Eppley Foundation.

Pages 24–25:
Study for *Dinner for Threshers*, 1934. Charcoal, graphite, and chalk on tan paper, 18 x 72 in. Private Collection.

Dinner for Threshers, 1934. Oil on hardboard, 19½ x 79½ in. Fine Arts Museums of San Francisco, Gift of Mr. And Mrs. John D. Rockefeller 3rd. 1979.7.105

Page 26:
(from top left to bottom right)
Grant Wood, c. 1920s. Cedar Rapids Museum of Art Archives.

Grant Wood, c. 1910. Cedar Rapids Museum of Art Archives.

Grant Wood with his McKinley Junior High School art students working on Imagination Isle Frieze, 1924. Cedar Rapids Museum of Art Archives.

Grant Wood, c. 1926. Cedar Rapids Museum of Art Archives.

Page 27:
(from top left to bottom right)
5 Turner Alley, north view, 2004. Cedar Rapids Museum of Art.

Interior view of 5 Turner Alley, looking east, c. 1925. Courtesy of Figge Art Museum, Grant Wood Archives.

Interior view of Grant Wood's "Mother's Hot Dog Stand" at 5 Turner Alley, c. 1925. Courtesy of Figge Art Museum, Grant Wood Archives.

Page 29:
5 Turner Alley Christmas Card, 1927. Relief print with hand coloring, pen and ink, 10 x 7¼ in. Cedar Rapids Museum of Art, Gift of John B. Turner II.